Bloom Bravely

Breanna Lowman

BookLeaf Publishing

India | USA | UK

Presentation by *BookLeaf Publishing*

Web: www.bookleafpub.com

E-mail: info@bookleafpub.com

ISBN: 9789360945190

First edition 2024

To all the dreamers who lift each other up. The world is big enough for all of us to contribute. Don't hold back, bloom bravely.

PREFACE

These poems are for anyone who has locked their words within a journal, for anyone who has kept their voice in a box, for all the creative souls drowning in fears, for all those who have questioned the importance of their own creations. I used to be you, before these words came to my heart and awakened me to an invitation. Before I let inspiration set my creative spirit free.

The words you write matter. The art you paint matters. The songs you sing matter. The stories you tell matter. You matter. And when you know that you matter, the confidence to share what is within you grows, like a flower. So, consider these words like water.

The time to be creative is now, dear ones.
Let go of perfection, reach out for connection.
Be brave enough to bloom.

I See You

I see you,
Sitting there in your sacred space
Warmed by the sparks of imagination
Burning with fire of inspiration
Content in your own world.

I see you and it is time,
Time for your fire to burn bright;
Embers radiating, flames growing
Add the kindling, the wind is blowing.

Feel the embrace
Creativity's flight
Rising with the light
Carrying you up and away.

It is time,
To share your little world
With the big beautiful world
Let yourself go,
You are no longer alone.

Flow

I am a river
pushed along by
divinity ever-flowing

Moved by the current of the spirit
abundant waters flow in words
speaking out as I scribe

Branches dip into the stream
receiving prose of refreshment
in thirst quenching mysteries

Light from above travels deep
flowers grow as identity takes root
in the ground of solid love

I shine. I reflect. I flow.
And so do you, don't you know?

Minnows Beneath Willows

The swimming minnows
beneath the willows
known for only being small.

The swimming minnows
are secret keepers
for much larger they can grow.

Oh, little minnow
known not for grandeur
don't let expectations win.

For you will surprise
surpass and rise
you are more than you appear.

Bloom

You were always a flower
planted in my garden
even when the time wasn't right
to bloom.

Your essence trapped within
for only you to enjoy
as waters nourished
and sunlight warmed.

But now your fragrance rises
out from your cocoon
the appointed time has come
for you to finally bloom.

Let the whole garden
take in your fragrance
as the wind spirit blows
revealing your radiance.

Dancing Bones

Meet me here
in the desert warmth
where I am
waiting for you.

I am a dry desert
a scorched plain
in need of rain
so I can bloom again,
rise above the wilt
open like a sunflower
stretching toward the sun.

Let silence find me
with a listening ear,
solitude greet me
with a knowing
that I am not alone.

Raise me up
out of this muck
where I lie dying,
lift my head
sing to my bones
to make them rise

and dance again.

Chase me down
with your love
until our hearts
are intertwined,
until healing comes
and humanity has become
all that we can be.

Light Runs Deep

down deep within
under darkness, shame
a flame of light
still burns bright

waiting, yearning
to break through
for chains to be broken
for freedom and liberation

you've punished yourself
for sins you think you are
purging yourself of darkness
yet still feel hated and lifeless

but you were never bad
at the core like they said
you don't deserve punishment
nor cruel diminishment

for in the beginning was light
and from light you were conceived
and the light was Love
you are more than you could dream of

unshakable identity
light woven into your DNA
goodness held within your heart
worth and value flow thru your veins

you are good and beautiful
that is who you are
though this truth can be hidden
it is never very far

for darkness is not
something you are
darkness tries to make hidden
all that you are

goodness runs deeper than evil
light deeper than darkness
may cleansing rain wash away
the dirt and shame
that has obscured
the truth of light within

Deeper Treasures Within

Waves crash upon the ocean floor
Creatures and hidden treasures swirl and dance
Sand dollars, shells, and pearls wash to shore
Gems and wonders from the deep expanse
Oceans full of things to awe at and adore

But you are worth so much more
Than the oceans' tide could bring in
You are worth more
You carry deeper treasures within

Deep underground caves unique in decor
Stalactites hang and stalagmites climb
Jewels and gemstones in crystal palaces stored
Mystery discovered in hidden places that shine
Caverns that beckon, come deep and explore

But you are worth so much more
Than the caves may all hold
You are worth more
You hold more value than silver and gold

A world beyond with symphonies to compose
Galaxies swimming in darkness vast
Energy and light hurled out into visual prose

Stars, moons, and planets like floating islands
entranced
Black holes keeping secrets nobody knows

But you are worth so much more
Than even the cosmos contain
You are worth more
You are more than anyone could ever explain

Canvas of the World

We are all paint from the same palette
Splattered on the canvas of the world
How dull it would be if we were all the same
color

A single color cannot paint a masterpiece
It's when shades of difference come together
That beauty dances and finds her way

There's no need to compare and compete
We are all part of the same art piece
Enhancing the belovedness of one other

Abundance

Blessings of abundance
Flow in with the tide
To gather at the feet of gulls
Who wade in the shallows
Dunking their heads underwater
To pick up hidden treasures.

The ocean, vast and deep
The storehouses of an abundant God
The gulls, waiting knee deep
To fill their stomachs, to meet their needs.

And I think of creativity
How it comes and goes
Of inspiration and intuition
How it moves and flows.

And I think of the gulls
Trusting in the tide
Not discouraged by the rock they grab
Nor dismayed by the empty shell of a crab
They simply toss it back and look again
Waiting to find the treasures
They know eventually
Will settle at their feet.

We can learn from the gulls
Expecting creativity to come
To flow in like the tide
Endlessly abundant inspiration
Just below our feet
Not hidden FROM us
But hidden FOR us
To find.

Will you seek it?

The Rhythm of Your Song

Light dances on ripples of reflected sky
Streams of zig-zagging shapes
Riding the water currents
Finding their way to where I am.

I welcome the patterns
As they break upon my bare feet
Hanging in the coolness
Below my dock sitting body.

I AM HERE,
Waiting on the edge.
LISTENING,
For you to speak.

Your voice is carried on the wind
You speak through the dazzling designs
Rippling across the lake
Changing in speed, design, direction

The current is taking you
Where you should go
You will get there
Where you are meant to be

The wind is your vehicle of speed
The heart behind your flow
The inspiration and rhythm
To the song your life sings

What do you want
Your journey to look like?
For that is ultimately
Up to you:

Frantic Traveler; worried and waiting, anxious
and alarmed
Peace Seeker; calm and joyful, expectant and
content
Wandering Cynic; impatient and bitter, apathetic
and unsatisfied
Adventure Taker; riding the flow with child-like
wonder

What is the rhythm of your life song?

Rise

look at the earth,
the trees, the water,
the needs that they meet
for us; human life

look at the earth,
the topsoil, rich in nutrient
able to conceive
from seed to nourish

basic needs met
on the basic level

dig deeper,
revealing stones and gems
discovering silver and gold
and ore for melting into metal

Something new
Something mold-able
Holding such potential

dig deeper,
finding dyes and pigments
uncovering raw materials

for sculpture and artwork

chemicals that change the dynamics
of how things work and function
life changing; exploration spurring
the chance to go beyond the imaginable

outside our sphere of understanding
rocket fuel to send us to space
connecting with the beyond
because we went to the core

dig deeper,
within ourselves
within our world

dig deeper,
within our culture
within our lives
within our hearts

dig deeper,
and we will find
that in digging deep
we actually rise

imagine what we could be
imagine the treasure still waiting to be found
within the core of each of us

dig a little deeper,
find creativity
bring it to the top
and rise

Renaissance

"Doing creativity lifts tiredness and creates the
energy for more creativity." -Lyn Lasneski

Renaissance
Oh the joy!
Reading, writing
Making music from noise

Renaissance
Come alive!
Dancing, singing
Through sunset and sunrise

Renaissance
Let creation rise!
Drawing and painting
Visions and stories of the wise

Renaissance
Springs of life come forth!
Imagination and creativity
Giving birth

Renaissance
Resistance to despair!

May all of us
Breath in the fresh air

You Look Like a Tomato

"Recognizing that people's reactions don't
belong to you is the only sane way to create."
-Elizabeth Gilbert, Big Magic

I remember the first time
I ran a timed mile
It was in middle school
And I ran like the wind

6 minutes 14 seconds
First in the whole class
Hot and sweaty and proud
My face beamed with joy

I got to my next class
Feeling good about myself
Until my teacher cast out words
That changed my life

"You look like a tomato!"
My teacher said
And the students laughed
Along with her

A seemingly innocent comment

Splintered into my teenage mind
The start of believing
Something is wrong with me
So I told myself:

Don't try so hard next time
Take it down a notch
Do everything you can
To hide the color of red
That can't seem to help
But bleed through
The skin of your cheeks

But no matter how I ran
How slow or how fast
In the heat or in the cool
My cheeks would blush
And a tomato I would become

The red of my face
Became the face of failure
The face of shame
The face of defeat

I stopped running.

Years and years later
While living abroad in China
I started running again

It was then that I received
A beautiful and unexpected gift
A redeeming comment
That washed away the wound

I had just gotten back from a long run
And I was red
Yes, I looked like a tomato
My friend saw me and said:

"Wow your face is amazing!
You have such good circulation!
My face never changes color!"

A different perspective
I had never thought of before
Because I was blinded by the shame
That the past had contained

But now I proudly claim:
I am not ashamed to look like a tomato!

When you see the red in my cheeks
I want you to know
This is the face of success
This is the face of hard work
This is a face worthy to be seen

Yes, I look like a tomato
Thank you for noticing.

Absolutely Everything

"You (create) in order to change the world,
knowing perfectly well that you probably can't,
but also knowing that ….the world changes
according to the way people SEE it, and if you
alter, even by a millimeter, the way people see
reality, then you can change it." -James Baldwin

Art, what is it good for?
Absolutely everything:

Art is a form of thinking
It invites us to look at life unblinking
      It's a wake up call to pay attention

Art is full of meaning
It is a new way of seeing
      It asks us to live with intention

Art keeps us evolving
On a path of problem solving
      It spurs us on to innovation

Art is a releasing of feelings
A road for inner healing
      It paves the way for revelation

It's a grand scheme revealing
      Pointing us toward beauty
It can set us off dreaming
      Beyond our daily duties

Art is the result of an unleashing
A releasing of inner creativity

And creativity can change the world

Meraki

"Work is love made visible." -Kahlil Gibran

It's a vocation of creation
starting with listening
to what your life is saying
about who you are and what you're about
inviting curiosity and wonder in
being comfortable within your own skin
creating is letting it all shine out.

When you love what you do
it's no longer work.
When you love what you do
you do it well.

It's a labor of love
encasing your heart in creativity
feeling alive to the work before you
allowing passion to leave your body
releasing your soul to embody
all that you bring forth
into the world.

When you love what you do
it's no longer work.

When you love what you do
you do it well.

When you work with love
success becomes insignificant.
When you work with love
you have learned a secret of life.

Nothing New

"There is nothing new under the sun."
-Ecclesiastes

The more podcasts I listen to, the more books
that I read
The more movies I watch, the more art that I see
I can't help but feel like there's nothing new to
say
So, what is the point of putting our stuff out
there anyway?

But what if it's not about having something new
to say
What if it's about rearranging ideas in different,
unique ways
Maybe some people are meant to hear us speak
Because there is no one else with these words
that they'll meet.

Maybe it's also about repetition
Words have the power to bring much needed
nutrition
We need to hear the same things over and over
When speaking to the heart, there's no such
thing as overexposure.

See, you don't need something new to say
To make what you have to say, valuable.
You just have to share what you feel you need to
Definitely for others, but most importantly for
you.

You've got to get it all out before you explode
All these questions and searching that come
from walking life's road
All these emotions, they've got to have
somewhere to go
There's got to be somewhere helpful it all can
go…

Art.
That's where it can go.
Because that's where it is never wasted.

Enchant Me

Bring me in
Take me close
Tell me a story
Strike a pose

I'll lean in
As you enchant
With magic words
You graciously grant

You are the story
I want to read
You are the muse
That makes my pen bleed

I'll be sucked in
Until the very end
As words are conceived
And connections transcend

Lotus Dancers

A winding dust trail
Circles the lotus pond
Traveled by many feet
Under the heat of the sun

Though on moonless nights
Paths disappear
And the trail becomes
A fearful place to tread

Tonight,
The pale moonlight
Illuminates the path
With tranquility

I walk alone
In reflection light
All responsibilities swept away
With the fragrance of the lotus flowers

Leaves of the lotus float above space
Like ballerinas swaying in the wind
Throwing white flowers like pearls
From their dancing artist hands

The breeze sweeps me up into the scene
The fragrance carries me to distant lands
Where the world is adorned in
Songs of beauty and stories sweet

Sailing Among Fireflies

In the dark of the night, unable to sleep
My gaze turns to the light, the moon too is
awake

I'm pulled up into space
the quintessence of the unknown
to sail among fireflies, to encounter grace
to float above gravity, a weightless embrace

Glorious light illuminates my mind
projections cast into the night skies
whirring, spinning vortex of thoughts
feelings flung out in galaxy blots

Too beautiful to behold
dreams too real not to feel

Yet pain, like gravity
keeps me grounded to humanity
pulling me back to reality

Where I am found
Where we are found

But there is always more

than gravity can contain
there is always more
than unrest and pain

Hope is the wind in my sail

Bubbles

Dream
Dream
Dream
I will meet you in your dreams

But dreaming found me scared
Scared of disappointment
Open to discouragement
For what if I dream so hard
And nothing comes to pass?

So, I ask the universe,
"How can I learn to hold dreams loosely?"
And the answer arrives as I watch
My kids play before my eyes
With their bubbles blowing by

Bubbles…
Let your dreams be like bubbles

Bubbles floating around your hand
Ideas waiting to pop and burst
They come and they go
Floating like inspiration gifts all around
Packages of wonder to be found

They are not all meant for you
But you are free to play with them too
Until the ones destined for you
Finally settle down

Play with the bubbles, it's okay if they pop
The bubble supply is never out of stock

Don't be afraid to dream, child
Embrace the bubble mess
See the reflected beauty
The glimpses of joy in a moment
From bubbles that float away
And bubbles that stay

Allow creativity to pop where it may
Experience the rush
Sense the blush
Feel the touch upon your skin
Hope is watching the horizon

The Call of the Microphone

Find your voice, I've heard it said
But mine has always been stuck in my throat
It cracks and it pops and has a mind of its' own
And when I try to sing it cuts off, breathless.
Silenced.

So, I'd sing in my room with a quiet voice
Where only my ears could hear the sound
And I'd write in a journal sealed and bound
So that in the waters of insecurity and fear I
wouldn't drown.

But every time I saw a microphone
It called out to me by name:

Come here and put your lips to me
Open your mouth and words will be waiting
Embrace the butterflies
And conquer the fears
Let your voice out
Let it ring clear
Your voice is meant to be heard
There is healing in your words.

So, I step up to the mic

Awkward as can be.

Gripping it with shaking arms
And a heart racing in between
And I open my mouth
And I hear my voice.

Echo and ring
Resound and reverberate
Bounce and resonate
Hover and soar.

I'm not afraid anymore.

www.ingramcontent.com/pod-product-compliance
Lightning Source LLC
Chambersburg PA
CBHW061728130726
47996CB00006B/2551